BLACK GIRL BLISS

Please

RADICAL SELF-CARE FOR
WILD WOMEN OF COLOR

PLEASE

Eleven25 Media
www.eleven25media.com

Copyright 2020. All Rights Reserved.

No part of this book may be reproduced by any process or recording, nor may it be stored, transmitted, or otherwise copied for public or private use (other than "fair use" as brief quotations for articles and reviews)
without prior written consent of the publisher.

This book is written to set you on the journey to empowerment and fulfillment. This book does not provide any medical advice or treatment of medical or emotional issues. Use of the techniques outlined in this book assumes personal responsibility on behalf of the reader/practitioner, not on the author or publisher.

1st Edition, August 2020

BOOKS BY BLACK GIRL BLISS

Pussy Prayers: Sacred and Sensual Rituals for Wild Women of Color

PLEASE

Dedication

Woman
With skin like the sky at winter midnight
Know that you may feel called to save this world
But <u>you must always save yourself first.</u>
Rest.
Set your burdens down.
Shed your layers, your titles, your
responsibilities.
Just be.
Sing a song, sip tea, stare out into space.
Ignore your marching orders.
They will be where you left them when you
return.
<u>Center self. Savor.</u>
<u>Be soft and still.</u>
<u>Bless the world with your presence when you
are ready.</u>
This time, with more power, more purpose,
more peace.
Please.

PLEASE

Contents

-PART ONE-

I.   Start Here

II.   Permission Granted

III.   The Power of Pleasure

IV.   Pleasure Activated

PLEASE

-PART TWO-

V. PLEASE: Affirmations, Meditations, and Rituals

VI. Resources

PART ONE

Start Here

CHAPTER ONE

PLEASE

I
Start Here

Dream with me for a moment.

See yourself in your mind's eye as the person you have always wanted to be. What does she look like? What does she wear? What does she do? How does she feel? What are her relationships like? What is her life like? How does it feel to be in her presence? In her home? How does it feel to see yourself in all your glory?

Good news! She already exists deep inside of you, waiting to be freed. We are going to make this dream come true.

In this book, we are going to journey together to becoming the person we want to be and creating the lives that we have always dreamed of, increasing our fulfillment and wellbeing through radical self-care and the power of pleasure. We'll discuss why pleasure matters, our complicated relationship with pleasure, how pleasure is the source of our power, and how to harness that power to create the life you desire and deserve.

Typically, when people hear the word pleasure they immediately think of sex, which isn't necessarily wrong, but we're going to go a little deeper than that.

PLEASE

Pleasure is the feeling of satisfaction, peace, ease, comfort, and enjoyment. That's it. That's the whole definition. No conditions, no exceptions. With this definition in mind, consider what brings you pleasure. How often do you experience pleasure? Is it situational? Do you only feel satisfaction and joy as a result of some event or circumstance, or can you conjure up the feeling naturally? Think of how you feel when you see a woman being free and going after what she wants with no shame. It might inspire you, but it might also make you uncomfortable because it's unfamiliar, and it reminds you of what you have not allowed yourself to do. Sit with these questions and ideas for a while and we'll revisit these later on.

Kicking the habit of self-neglect makes a major difference in our lives and the lives of others; it is a significant improvement that we would not have known was possible had we not been introduced to people who inspire us and resources like this book and others that proclaim pleasure as a natural state of being and a life-changing necessity. We are reclaiming our right and responsibility to pursue pleasure, and in doing so, we must unpack the reasons why we feel like we don't deserve to enjoy life. What are we holding on to that makes us feel that we are unworthy of goodness? What myths do we believe about feeling good, taking care of ourselves, and the pursuit of satisfaction and joy? How have those beliefs prevented us from truly knowing pleasure for ourselves? Who benefits from

PLEASE

us denying ourselves pleasure and sacrificing our wellbeing for others?

Why Pleasure?

We are created from pleasure. The moment of orgasm is what began our development into the people we are today. Thus, pleasure is our natural state of being. When we stray too far from pleasure for too long, we find ourselves burnt out, overwhelmed, overworked, stressed, and exhausted. When we do not care for ourselves through ensuring that we experience consistent joy and peace, we see the symptoms of dis-ease within our bodies, minds, and spirits.

When you're feeling cared for, revitalized, nourished, and restored, while also experiencing satisfaction on a regular basis, you are unstoppable. You have the energy to do, be, and have everything that you want. So why is it that we've been trained to recharge our electronic devices more than we recharge our bodies, minds, and spirits? As we understand more about the link between pleasure and power, we understand why we have been denied and discouraged from prioritizing pleasure for so long.

Black women, particularly descendants of enslaved Africans, have been in survival mode since we were abducted from our homes and stranded in foreign lands. Trauma has been passed down generation after generation with little context and fewer resources with which to heal. We continue to live under the direct threat of violence as the entire world makes clear how much they hate both Blackness and

PLEASE

womanhood. How is anyone supposed to find pleasure in that?

   Joy is unusual to many of us. We are suspicious of and sometimes irritated by people who seem "too happy". We second guess and chastise ourselves when we exceed our usual levels of contentment. We feel unworthy, unsure of how long it will last, and wonder what people will think of us being so happy. We've been taught that pleasure is not for us and that the pursuit of pleasure is frivolous and irresponsible. When we attempt to be free and move towards what interests and delights us, we're discouraged from it and taunted for our desires. If we tell someone we're interested in pursuing something that brings us pleasure, people will often tell us "that's some white people shit" or "that's for rich people with trust funds." Why do we consider pleasure as something reserved for those with the highest levels of privilege?

We have inherited roles and responsibilities as dictated by the people who raised us, and the people who raised them, and the people who raised them, who were seeking to negate rampant stereotypes about Black people and protect themselves from the consequences of these stereotypes being considered true. We must be productive. We must not sleep too long or laze about. We must wake up with the sun. We can't waste the day. Get up, get dressed, get busy. We dare not spend the day in bed unless we are seriously ill. We must be strong. We must put on a brave face. We must say we're fine when asked how we're doing.

PLEASE

Whether we are up or down, we cannot be honest about what we're going through. We should be happy to be here, happy to work hard, happy to serve, no matter what.

Despite this, our mothers and grandmothers found ways to prioritize their pleasure, even if it seemed that they were lacking the typical resources for them to be able to do so. What do you think your mother did when she put you to bed? The answer is most likely *whatever she wanted to do*. This was her time to indulge in what made her feel cared for and at peace. Your grandmother had her rituals, her favorite foods and drinks, her "stories" and other TV shows that she watched in her favorite spot in her living room. She woke up before the sun to pray, adorn herself, and eat a delicious meal in silence before the rest of the house arose. This was her pleasure. We have always found ways to do or have something that we enjoyed, something that was just for us.

This book is just an introduction, a starting point, and just one piece amongst many works that explore the power and importance of pleasure. As the elders say, "there is nothing new under the sun." Information presented here is not new, but it is a collection of wisdom and remembrance of who we have been and who we are called to be. Use this book to practice feeling comfortable prioritizing and feeling pleasure, to learn what truly satisfies you, and to be unapologetic in pursuit of those things.

PLEASE

The Problem with "Self-Care"

Mainstream media has presented self-care to us as commercialized, money-driven indulgences in things like spa days and shopping and vacations. This illusion of self-care perpetuates the idea that we can only be soothed from stress through buying something or spending time elsewhere. What does this do for people who don't have the luxury of extra money or extra time? People deal with being shamed for not being able to participate in these experiences, being told they need to take care of themselves but not given the tools to be able to do so. Additionally, the mainstream self-care movement ignores how women in general and Black women in particular live under societal, systemic stressors that cannot be fixed with bubble baths and bottomless mimosas.

To be radical means to be dedicated to changing the fundamental nature of something, to do something in a way that has not been done before, or in a way that returns to its root — its most natural state. By exploring pleasure as radical self-care, we develop a way of practicing physical, mental, and spiritual wellbeing through activities and rituals that are proactive, holistic, sustainable, and accessible. Writer and activist Audre Lorde said that caring for herself was an act of political warfare, particularly in the face of a society that has shown how much it does not care about Black women. Prioritizing and pursuing pleasure is the most comprehensive, effective, and realistic form of self-care as it allows to us

PLEASE

to nourish and restore ourselves in a way that shopping sprees and manicures could never do. Caring for ourselves by engaging only in what satisfies us is revolutionary because it goes against everything that we are taught by a heteronormative, patriarchal, capitalist society that expects us to be machines and ignore our needs and natural inclinations. Through this work, we are reimagining what it means to care for ourselves and dreaming up new ways of living and being that put ourselves and our joy first.

Rules for This Work

Rule One: If you are reading this book, it is safe to assume that you are ready (or at least mildly interested) in caring for yourself by creating more pleasure in your life. This book requires deep examination and unlearning of our aversion to feeling good and relearning how to care for ourselves in a way that brings us back to center — back to who we really are. As is the case with all matters of personal development, nothing will work unless you do. You cannot expect results from work you haven't committed to or completed. If you are serious about enhancing your wellbeing through pleasure, then you have to be willing to do

PLEASE

what is required. Pursuing pleasure is all fun and games until it demands that you confront your self-sacrificing behavior and hold yourself accountable for the part you have played in your own discomfort and mistreatment. This work requires discipline to be effective. Stay the course. It will all be worth it.

Rule Two: There is no excuse to sprinkle sugar on shit. You should not have to dig deep and reach far to prove that something brings you joy. You will need to examine what satisfies you in the long-term, what soothes you in the moment, and what you engage in that has long-term consequences. You'll need to be honest about the things you say you enjoy but you really don't, and all the times you say "yes" to things when you really want to say "no." We will discuss establishing and maintaining boundaries as a means of self-care. It is up to you to realize when you are engaging in people, places, and things that are depleting your time, energy, attention, and resources.

Rule Three: There is no one-size-fits-all to pleasure. We are letting go of the notion that pleasure is "guilty" or that everyone should experience pleasure in the same ways. This is a process of relearning and accepting your own uniqueness. Do not feel pressured to do anything that other people are doing just because it's popular or socially acceptable.

Rule Four: Use your common sense. If something doesn't feel right, if some piece of information doesn't sit well with your

PLEASE

spirit, acknowledge that. Do not ignore it. Develop and listen to your intuition so you can make choices in your best interest without harming yourself or others.

Things to Note

As is always the case with content created by the Black Girl Bliss platform, this book is written for self-identified Black women and femmes by a Black woman. I know that other people will read my books and they are certainly welcome to do so. However, my passion, my loyalty, and my talents will always be used for the purpose of serving Black women, femmes, and girls first and foremost, because we share many of the same experiences and beliefs that we must process and unlearn so that we can be our best selves. Standing at the intersection of various systems of oppression, we deserve the space and undivided attention to get our shit together away from the gaze and input of others who could never truly grasp what we deal with. Contained in these pages are conversations that only members of our diverse yet indestructibly linked sisterhood can fully understand. Other people who read this are welcome to tap into what they are able to access from this book, but its language, depictions, and knowledge all draw from Black feminine experiences.

   Black Girl Bliss is an educational platform dedicated to Black women's wellbeing and fulfillment through the power of pleasure. Whether the topic is sexuality, spirituality, or self-care (three main gateways to pleasure — we'll get to

PLEASE

this later), the topics and ideas shared in books by BGB will overlap. Pleasure is pleasure, whether it comes from sex or sleep or wading barefoot through a creek. That said, you may see the same ideas repeated in every BGB book; that is intentional. Repetition and practice are how we learn.

As is also the case with books by BGB, you do not have to read this book in the order in which it is written. Feel free to skip around to different chapters and sections based on your interests and needs. Each chapter contains a short summary of the main points and the most important messages and themes will be repeated throughout the book (again, this is intentional), so don't worry about missing anything important by not reading this book from first page to last, one paragraph after another.

Throughout this book, we will discuss the consequences of denying ourselves pleasure on our physical, mental, and spiritual wellbeing. This is not to imply or explicitly cite any clinical diagnosis or prescriptions. Pleasure is a practice of putting yourself and your needs first. If you find that your needs go beyond what you can figure out on your own, please seek professional counseling and medical treatment.

While we move toward a vision of ourselves whose lives embody all that we desire and deserve, part of the work explored here will require you to take responsibility for your current life situation and make changes as needed. This work in no way ignores the systemic

PLEASE

oppression that we face as Black women: racism, sexism, capitalism, poverty, misogynoir, ableism, ageism, colorism, homophobia, transphobia, and more. Instead, this work asks you to find the areas of your life where you can subvert these systems and the beliefs they have imparted on us for so long and to be accountable for making the changes that are in your power to make.

Lastly, it would be irresponsible, dishonest, and downright disrespectful if I did not acknowledge that Black women live under systems intentionally designed to keep us exhausted and without basic necessities. Our disconnection from pleasure serves these systems as they seek to ensure that we "stay in our place", working and producing on demand. Many of us do not have the time, money, or support that we deserve, and we certainly are not looking to do anything that uses up more resources than it provides. I believe that anything that has been intentionally designed can be intentionally redesigned, and this book aims to assist Black women and femmes at all ages and stages to create lifestyles that best serve them, their needs, and their desires. This book will only suggest free or low-cost and accessible ways to engage in self-care through pleasure. Writing this, I am keeping in mind the women who work double and triple shifts to make ends meet, the mothers who don't have anyone who can take their kids for a weekend, and the young folks just starting out and trying to find their way. It is my hope that you find this book helpful in adding

PLEASE

realistic and effective methods of self-care into your arsenal.

Pressure Points

The Pressure Points in this book are questions to help you reflect on your current state as well as your progress as you work through your relationship to pleasure. Move through each section of this book with these questions in mind. Be sure to write down your responses to these questions somewhere private and easily accessible. To keep track of your growth, notice how your responses to these questions change as your relationship to pleasure changes.

Additional resources and prompts to aid you on this journey are in Part Two of this book.

What do you believe about pleasure?

Do you believe you deserve pleasure?

How easily can you imagine and engage in pleasure outside of your sexuality?

How does the idea of putting yourself first make you feel?

Where in your life do you see the connection between pleasure and power?

PLEASE

These questions focus on feeling, which means that you will need to be able to tap into your inner self to get to a true understanding of your emotions and beliefs around self-care and pleasure. It is important that you name your feelings as often and as specifically as you can so that you can become more in tune with the things your body, mind, and spirit are telling you, and begin your journey to healing any emotions, underlying thoughts, and experiences that don't feel good.

In order to do this work, you cannot be afraid to feel deeply, whether the emotion feels good or bad, easy or uncomfortable. Remember that you will eventually get to the other side of that feeling and can grow from there with the knowledge you gained through the shadows, up into the light.

The Denial of Pleasure

Our negative beliefs around self-care and pleasure didn't come out of thin air. Instead, they have been insidiously planted there by people and institutions who are terrified of our freedom, intimidated by our power, and benefit from our miseducation and suffering.

Prior to the colonial invasion of our native homelands, we were free to adorn ourselves as we pleased, move our bodies in ways that felt good, and express ourselves in the ways that were instinctive to us. When the imperialist colonizer gaze fell upon us, we became objects of both lust and disgust. Our ways of expression

PLEASE

and celebrations of ourselves were mocked, called barbaric, and punished by those who thought that we should be their property. We were hyper-sexualized starting from young ages and subjected to physical and mental violence just for being our magnificent selves. We were struck down for seeming too proud, too confident, or too smart. We quickly learned that it was no longer safe for us to be as we had always been. It was easier and certainly safer to not call attention to ourselves, to be still, solemn, silent. To shrink ourselves as small as possible. To be invisible. We hoped that modesty and hard work would shield us from the violence from people who claimed to hate us and still desired us at the same time. We watched others be praised for being meek and mild, doing only as they were told, and we learned to emulate that behavior in hopes that we would be spared from harm. Being productive provided some sense of safety and security. And even after all of this denial of our pleasure — our joy, our comfort, our peace, our ease — we were still considered dangerous, uncivilized, and in need of being controlled.

Fast-forward to today and you'll find that many of the things our ancestors had to do to survive became ingrained beliefs about how we should behave in order to be safe. We still believe, on some level, that our bodies must be controlled, covered, and of a socially acceptable size in order to be regarded as attractive, respectable, or worthy of protection. We dare not call too much attention to ourselves or celebrate ourselves out loud

PLEASE

for fear of being seen as vain and in need of restraint (which we typically call "being humble"). Being emotional or expressing our feelings does not feel safe, so we suppress our feelings and disconnect from those feelings in our bodies. We have trouble listening to our own wants and needs because they don't feel "obedient" to whatever authorities we still feel we must answer to. We still believe overworking is our best means of safety and security. We cannot talk about the things that bring us joy without feeling some discomfort and cannot lean into those things we love without feeling guilt and shame. We believe that the only respectable use of our bodies is for production, and we are always waiting to be punished for being too free.

We know we deserve better. We dream of more. We are determined to change the trajectory for ourselves, our children, and their children. Through the reclamation of our pleasure, we can engage in a practice of self-care that feels natural to us and serves us best.

You're Here for a Reason

The fact that you are reading these words means that you are interested in reimagining the way that you care for yourself. You are already releasing the expectations of your behavior set upon you by a society that would rather you remain silent and subservient. You know that there is a better way to move through life than the way most of us have been taught. You are ready to learn ways to

PLEASE

restore and revive yourself when you need it. You are ready to feel good, not just on occasion, but most often.

As you begin this journey, be gentle with yourself, remain open, stay accountable for your growth, and move forward with the intention that you will rediscover what has been hidden and denied from you for so long. Life is the longest thing we will ever do in this physical realm. Why not make sure it's satisfying?

Pleasure Principles

- Pleasure is the feeling of satisfaction, peace, ease, comfort, and enjoyment.
- Prioritizing and pursing pleasure is the most comprehensive, effective, and realistic form of self-care as it allows us to nourish and restore ourselves so that we have the energy to be, do, and have all that we desire and deserve.
- Pleasure involves more than just sex, and our discomfort with feeling good is the result of being mocked and punished for engaging our natural inclinations.
- This book is an introduction, not an encyclopedia, and presents ideas that may not be new but are important to remember.
- Be gentle with yourself on this journey.

PLEASE

Permission Granted

CHAPTER TWO

PLEASE

II
Permission Granted

How do you know that you are in need of more comfort, joy, ease, and satisfaction in your life? You find yourself operating on autopilot, going through the motions day after day. You feel numb or have a hard time expressing any emotion. You cannot delight in the good things in your life because you don't believe you deserve them, or you are waiting for something terrible to happen next. You feel anxious and guilty for resting or saying no to things you don't have the interest or energy to do. You feel like life is passing you by and you have nothing to show for it. You often feel envious of other people's freedom, accomplishments, and opportunities. You're exhausted, burnt out, and overwhelmed. You're not sleeping well. You're always rushing and feeling pressed for time. You have just enough energy to make sure you and the people you are responsible for survive, and no more than that. You find reasons to judge and gossip about other people because it makes you feel better about your own life. You complain about your life but do little to change it. There always

PLEASE

seems to be drama around you, or you always have "a lot going on." You seek to gain and maintain control over people and situations because you feel like you cannot control the trajectory of your own life.

The first step to moving from surviving to thriving is choosing yourself, regardless of the other obligations you might have. This doesn't mean neglecting your kids or not going to work or anything else that would be irresponsible and put you in a worse position. Choosing yourself means making sure your needs are met before attending to anyone or anything else. How much good can you be for the people that rely on you when you can't be good to yourself? Prioritizing pleasure means prioritizing your wellbeing, your happiness, and your safety. The moment you decide to prioritize your wants and needs is the moment you begin to thrive.

When I graduated college and decided I would become a teacher, I was so excited. I had been working with children since I was in high school and I wanted to recreate my own idyllic elementary school experience. I was proud of my decision to teach. Though I knew I wouldn't make as much money as my peers who had pursued other fields, the social affirmation that came from telling people "I'm going to be a teacher" felt validating. People were proud of me. My family couldn't wait to tell anyone who would listen that their daughter/granddaughter/niece/cousin was going to teach school. I knew that this was a field I would enjoy and do well in, which seemed to me to be the best marker

PLEASE

of post-graduate success. I felt like I was doing the right thing.

Fast-forward to my first year in the classroom and I was absolutely miserable. It was nothing like I thought it would be. I was constantly being told that I was an ineffective teacher despite the exponential growth of my students. I knew I was giving my students what they needed, but what they needed didn't align with what the school administrators wanted to see. Being fired for insubordination and incompetence was a constant threat. I felt gaslighted and unsupported, and the situation never got better. I wanted to quit every single day, but I could not help but think about all the people who were so proud of me. I didn't want to lose that validation and praise, but I didn't feel good about my life or my work. The disconnect between the improvements I saw my students making and the poor evaluations I was receiving from my school's principals made me doubt myself and my abilities. The long hours of grading student work, writing lessons, conferencing with parents, team meetings, and everything else that teaching entails was wearing me out. On top of all that, I was a full-time graduate student in order to earn my state teacher certification. There was just too much on my plate and I had never experienced this level of overwhelm before.

    After only a month or so in the classroom and through the rest of my teaching career, I hated going to work. I had watched my mother work the same job my entire life and she always hated it. No adult I knew particularly enjoyed their

PLEASE

job, even if they were good at what they did. Other young teachers at my school would be in tears by the end of the week and the few veteran teachers among us seemed to move through the hallways in an apathetic daze. I began to think that hating your job was to be expected as a young professional. My anxiety made me nauseous and gripped my chest tightly every Sunday night and every weekday morning. I came home after work and just slept. I didn't go out on weekends like a person in their early twenties usually does. From Friday afternoon to Sunday night, my biggest adventure was moving from my bed to my couch. I started to have thoughts about myself and my life that really scared me. I knew I couldn't keep living this way, but I didn't know I had permission to do anything differently.

My journey to pleasure has been messy and full of mistakes. I had to pivot many times to get it right, but I was and am committed to creating a life that truly satisfies me. Though it seems like a contradiction, caring for yourself through the pursuit of pleasure won't always feel good. It will require emotional work, shedding stereotypes and rejecting internalized judgements from other people. It will require you to be honest with yourself, to try and fail, to have difficult conversations, to create and maintain boundaries, to break bad habits, to leave things behind, and to make peace with the past so that you can move forward. You will have to sit with your deepest self, your shadow self, and fully immerse yourself in the journey of healing in order to stand firmly and confidently in

PLEASE

the grandest vision for yourself and your life. Had I not made the changes I needed to make to feel good, I am not certain I would be here doing what I'm doing, writing this book and looking around at some of my wildest dreams and most fervent prayers come true.

    You are accountable for your life and the things you can control. You are responsible for your wellbeing and your pleasure. You can choose to change your life at any point, any moment, any age, and in any position. These changes start in the mind first. Changing your habits through changing your beliefs about your capabilities and your worthiness is half the battle. Start by practicing the belief that your satisfaction is just as important as your responsibilities, and that your joy is just as essential as your obligations. You can and you must pursue and prioritize pleasure now. You do not have to wait for some perfect moment in your life or a perfect version of yourself in order to experience satisfaction, joy, and ease on a regular basis.

Prioritizing Pleasure

On an episode of The Oprah Winfrey Show, Oprah told an audience of mostly women that they should put themselves first on their list of priorities and they booed her. Oprah was visibly shocked as she did not expect that response from the audience. She didn't think she had said anything wrong. Why did they boo her? Because they believed the myths they were taught about what it meant to put themselves first and prioritize pleasure.

PLEASE

We have been taught through every cultural institution (family, school, most religions, media, etc.) that sacrificing yourself for others is something we should strive for, something that all the best people do. Through this lens, putting yourself before others is controversial and almost taboo. This is one reason why prioritizing and pursuing pleasure is radical. It calls for us to shift an entire cultural paradigm about what it means to be a good person, partner, parent, child, and friend.

Ignoring our own needs and giving all that we have to others is not sustainable, and Black women have been the ones largely harmed by this expectation. We work ourselves to the bone and put everyone before ourselves until we exhaust ourselves and die. We are trained to be help-meets and praised for our selflessness and strength for holding it all together. However, the greatest love we can show for others is being our best selves for them. What would happen if you told your loved ones that you care about them so much that you insist on being the person that they deserve by putting yourself first? If you can't do it for yourself, do it for the young people who are looking at you as an example. What do you want to pass on to them? Knowing that they are looking to you for what adulthood should be or look like, what would you show them instead?

    The pursuit and prioritization of pleasure is the kind of self-care that radiates out to everything in your universe, changing everything it touches for the better. Evaluate how your life feels and

PLEASE

what is in your power to do differently. This is how we develop and maintain our personal power that gives us the energy to do, be, and have everything that we could ever dream of.

What Pleasure Is and What Pleasure Is Not

Pursuing pleasure in the name of radical self-care is not an excuse to harm yourself or others. It is not permission to disregard other people, their feelings, their needs, and their right to pleasure. Putting yourself, your satisfaction, and your joy first does not mean that you ignore your responsibilities or the people, places, and things that rely on you for their wellbeing. Pleasure is not only about sex, nor is it only found within grooming and pampering practices like manicures and bubble baths. Pleasure is not something you can purchase and does not require any product or service. Pleasure should not empower you to indulge in vices and habits to the point of self-harm. Pleasure is not just for people with extra resources or certain levels of privilege. Pleasure is not found in any activity we feel obligated to participate in to feel loved or accepted. Pleasure is not a waste of time nor is it irresponsible. Pleasure is not synonymous with or always followed by pain. While we can give thanks to our pain for helping us to know pleasure and making our joy even more sweet, we do not have to subject ourselves to continuous mistreatment and harm in order to know pleasure.

Pleasure is joy, satisfaction, ease, comfort, and peace. Pleasure is power.

PLEASE

Pleasure is resistance against systems created to break our bodies and minds. Pleasure is rest. Pleasure is justice. Pleasure is productive. Pleasure is protection. Pleasure is resilience in the face of suppression, denial, and violence. Pleasure is a practice. Pleasure is gracious. Pleasure is fun. Pleasure is a weapon to fight life's battles and a balm to soothe life's wounds. Pleasure is essential. Pleasure is liberation.

Self-Care vs. Self-Soothing

Sometimes, life just sucks, and you can't be bothered to think deeply about what brings you pleasure. All you know is that you feel bad, and you want to feel better immediately. This is when we tend to self-soothe, turning to anything that will make us feel less bad in the least amount of time. Self-soothing can look like binge watching a TV show, having a drink or two (or three), indulging in comfort foods, grooming and pampering practices, or purchasing something nice for yourself. Self-soothing is natural, and it is a way for us to get out of our funk so that we can think clearly again. Once we regain some clarity, we can more intentionally engage in true self-care, typically by establishing ways to avoid or lessen our interaction with those people, places, and things that made us feel bad in the first place.

When we are trying to quiet those uncomfortable and sometimes painful feelings, we might reach for activities and habits like smoking, drinking, drugs, foods that our minds and mouths love but our bodies do not, people that *certain* body

PLEASE

parts of ours love but our hearts and minds do not — you get the picture. To engage in these things is not a failure on your part. You are no less mature, intelligent, spiritual, or anything else because you turned to easily accessible ways of feeling good.

  Our methods of soothing our hurt feelings have a place, but we cannot rely on self-soothing alone to bring us back to center. When we only reach for the quick fixes without sitting with our emotions, figuring out what we need to do for ourselves to support our grounding and growth and ensure our comfort, ease, and joy in the long-term, we can do more harm to ourselves than good. We may find that we are overindulging in avoidant and distracting activities that only provide temporary distraction and relief to fill the void of joy and satisfaction in our lives, using these sometimes detrimental coping mechanisms we have developed to escape our hurt feelings, and never actually addressing the root cause for more permanent and sustainable solutions. When we continue to neglect caring for ourselves, we can be less kind, less patient, and feel angry, desperate, or hopeless toward changing our current life situation, which can lead to anxiety, depression, substance abuse, and certain types of self-harm. You must be self-aware enough to determine your motivation behind your behavior. Will it bring you quick comfort for ten minutes or will it bring you deep joy for ten years? Is it real, radical self-care, or is it just temporarily masking your craving for pleasure?

PLEASE

Goodbye, Guilt!

If you ask anyone about their "guilty pleasures" you'll hear about the things they enjoy but feel ashamed of based on how they think people will perceive them. Other than folks who take pleasure in violent and inhumane activities, no one should be ashamed of the things that bring them satisfaction and joy. That's not to say you have to shout the things you love from the rooftops or tell every living soul about what you like to do during your "me time." It is perfectly normal to keep some things private, especially when those things are deeply personal or hold sacred meaning to you. Let go of the stigma and shame attached to things that you like that others may think are ridiculous, childish, strange, or don't seem to fit your public image or persona. All of us have things that bring us joy that would have the exact opposite effect for another person. Pleasure is a deeply personal experience, and there is nothing guilty about it.

Another way we often experience guilt and shame around pursuing pleasure is when we buy in to the idea that any time that we spend on ourselves and not in service of something or someone else is time wasted. We have been led to believe that our value is determined through our service and our productivity. You may have even had someone call you selfish when you were young because you wouldn't give them something of yours that they wanted, and it probably made you feel bad because we think of "selfish" as a negative label, something you never want to be called. We've been taught that

· PLEASE

to desire things just for yourself is also selfish but wanting more for yourself does not mean you are ungrateful for what you currently have. You do not have to settle for what is given to you just because things could be worse. What you desire for yourself does not have to be based on what the people around you have or desire for themselves. You have the right to ask for and go after exactly what you want, and you are always allowed to want more, better, or different at any point in time. As you pursue pleasure, become comfortable with the idea of being selfish with your time, your attention, your energy, and your resources.

Remember when I said that my journey of pursuing pleasure was messy and full of mistakes? Well, I dealt with a lot of guilt when I finally made the decision to leave the classroom. My family couldn't believe I would quit my job that, to them, I should have been in for the next 30 years until I retired. Who was I to think I didn't have to deal with a job that I hated when that seemed to be the norm? Well, that didn't stop me from dreaming of a life where "work" was easy, fun, and honestly, *optional*. I ventured down several rabbit holes looking for ways to make my life and work feel good. I thought maybe if I went back to school and trained for another career, things might be better. Maybe if I changed my aesthetic to match the girls who seemed like they were having all the fun on social media, I might feel better. Maybe if I lost weight, maybe if I had longer hair, maybe if I had different friends or lived in a different place…maybe…maybe…maybe.

PLEASE

The culmination of all those "maybes" resulted in me essentially hitting rock bottom. I had nothing to show for myself and all my exploring, and naturally, I felt guilty. I was ashamed that I had to ask for help to keep myself afloat because I had quit my job. I was ashamed that I had this grand plan to change my life and it just wasn't working out. I was ashamed that I was no closer to figuring out what truly brought me joy than I was when I was still teaching. I watched all these people who were so proud of me when I was a teacher start to gossip about me as I was floundering from one thing to the next. I started to believe that maybe it wasn't in the cards for me to have all these things I desired. I started applying for teaching jobs because it seemed like my only option, but the idea of having to go back to that environment gave me more of those very scary thoughts that I'd had before.

What I hadn't realized at the time was that even though I wanted more for myself and my life, I hadn't taken the time to think through what actually made me feel excited and fulfilled. I was going after the things that other people who seemed satisfied with their lives were doing. I was trying to crawl my way into spaces that didn't fit me, but they fit so many other people that I thought I just had to make it work. It took some time to understand that I was attempting to build a life that I had never seen before. I didn't have any examples of what I was trying to do, so I had to follow this uncharted path to pleasure all by myself and be unapologetic in pursuing the things that delighted me

PLEASE

regardless of what other people thought of me. When I figured this out, the world opened to me and everything I needed and wanted became clear.

If I had never started down the path to ensuring that I was caring for myself in a way that was truly empowering and restorative, if I had remained in those spaces that I didn't fit in because I felt guilty and ashamed of being "selfish," I would have never written a book that helped so many Black women and femmes feel seen and heard, giving them the courage to begin healing and understanding their right to pleasure. Where are you allowing guilt and shame to keep you from what you really want, knowing that there are so many people who will be blessed by you standing in your "selfishness" and following your bliss?

Unlearning and Relearning

Most of us have grown up in a culture that has made us deeply uncomfortable with the idea of loving ourselves and celebrating the things we love about ourselves out loud. We are not allowed to be "full of ourselves" or like ourselves too much. We were taught to be "humble," and that we should not be too proud because the things we are prideful about can always be taken away. We risk making others feel bad if they don't have what we have or love themselves the way we love ourselves. Women who take pleasure in their bodies and their beauty are called "vain." Women who celebrate themselves

PLEASE

and their accomplishments are accused of "bragging." Some of us have trouble even accepting compliments because we have been so indoctrinated in the idea that we should not think highly of ourselves.

    I was blessed to have incredibly high self-esteem as a child. I received high praise from the adults in my life, especially as it pertained to academics. My mother surrounded me with people, art, and literature that uplifted and celebrated Black womanhood. I never questioned the beauty of my dark brown skin or my full lips and nose because everyone around me had the same features. Strangely, though, whenever I would look in the mirror and say, "I look pretty!" or when I'd do well on a school assignment and say something like, "I'm so smart!" I was scolded and accused of being vain. Throughout my childhood, teachers and other adults in my life would call me things like "cavalier" and try to find ways to "put me in my place." I didn't understand their disdain for me when I hadn't done anything but be self-confident and aware of my abilities. My mother would frequently tell me that I needed to be quiet and let someone else praise me because saying it myself, about myself, would make people dislike me.

 Well, it's a good thing I have never been a fan of doing as I was told. I knew, even as a child, that if I waited for other people to compliment me in order to celebrate myself, I could be waiting forever to hear the truth about myself. I knew that if no one praised or celebrated me, it didn't mean that I was not all the things I knew myself to be. They simply didn't recognize

PLEASE

it, which was none of my business. I didn't think that I was prettier or smarter than anyone else. I wasn't saying these things to put anyone else down. I didn't even say things like this very often, but that's just how uncomfortable it made the adults around me. Why was it wrong for me to celebrate what I knew to be true and had certain proof of? Why did I have to be concerned with what other people thought of what I thought of myself? As an adult now, I realize that the adults around me had probably never considered that they had permission to love themselves out loud the way I did, or that they would even be worthy of praise just for being who they were.

    Who does it serve for you not to think highly of yourself? Who taught you to be "humble," and why? I believe that harmful religious ideologies that tell people they are "wretched" and "unclean" coupled with large corporations that market their products and services to us by convincing us that something is wrong with us are the main culprits as to why the celebration of our fullest selves makes us uncomfortable. We are collectively experiencing lack in our feelings of worthiness. We do not believe that we deserve good things or praise. Through radical self-care, we are releasing unworthiness and the idea that to love and admire ourselves is negative. We are making it a habit to celebrate ourselves, our bodies, and our lives through pleasure.

PLEASE

Ask for What You Want

Something I had to relearn in my early adulthood was that I had to ask for what I wanted, or I would not get it. I realized that my feelings were always hurt because I was waiting for someone to do something for me and they didn't, not because they didn't think I was worthy, but because I didn't make my needs and desires known. Why didn't they invite me? Why didn't they pick me? Why didn't they help me? The idea that I needed to actually speak up and say something didn't clearly occur to me until I met a certain coworker at my second job out of college. We'll call her Lana. Lana is a Black woman just a few years older than me. Her appearance is striking, as she has gorgeous dark skin and big brown eyes.

She was always personable, funny, helpful, and very expressive. You could hear her talking, laughing, or singing the latest Drake song no matter where she was in the office. She had a positive rapport with everyone, and people often looked to her for leadership. She had been with the company for almost five years before I got there, and though we had the same entry-level position, it was clear that she was running the show around there.

What struck me most about Lana was how she was never afraid to ask for what she wanted and because of that, she usually got exactly what she asked for. At one of our first team meetings, I brought the remainder of my lunch with me to the conference room — a small bag of grapes and a granola bar. Lana came into the room and sat next to me. About halfway

PLEASE

through the meeting, Lana whispers to me, "Girl, those grapes look so good. Can I have a few?" I quickly grabbed the bag and poured three or four grapes into her hand and she thanked me. This innocent exchange caught me off guard, not because she had asked for my grapes but because she had no shame in asking for something she saw and wanted. I would have never had the courage to ask anyone for something they had that looked good to me. As she and I worked together over the course of the year that I was with the company, I saw Lana asking for what she wanted time and time again and almost always getting it. Lana would ask the CEO for meetings to get advice on the company Lana was starting, and the CEO met with her. Lana would ask to work from the coffee shop next door to our building instead of at her desk, and her supervisor honored her request. Lana asked to use our office to host her own company's event on a Saturday, and she was given the key to the front door and the code to the security system. I loved that she was not only unashamed of asking but seemingly unafraid of possible rejection. Lana asked for things that made me gasp and clutch my proverbial pearls, not because anything she asked for was inappropriate, but because she boldly asked for things that I didn't even think I had the authority or agency to request. She asked for things that never occurred to me that I could have.

    I don't know the secret for Lana getting what she wanted. She wasn't a high-powered boss within the company, she wasn't the most senior employee, and she

PLEASE

was not the oldest person in the building. We definitely did not work for some generous and benevolent company (that's a story for another time). All I know is that I was inspired by the way she got what she asked for, how she was never concerned about what people would think of her boldness, and that I needed to adopt some of that bravery and tenacity in my own life.

Be like Lana. You have permission to ask for what you want directly from the person who can give it to you. You may be surprised by just how much you receive when you finally open your mouth.

Stay Juicy. Share Your Overflow.

You've probably heard the saying that goes something like, "You cannot pour from an empty cup; you must fill your cup up first." Essentially, this means that you can't give to others if you don't have anything for yourself. But this phrase implies that you must give away what you have, which is not true. When you are renewed and revitalized through caring for yourself, all of that energy is for you and you only. What's in your proverbial cup is yours. Our goal is to stay full, hydrated, and juicy, and we do that through engaging in the things that bring us pleasure. How can you stay satisfied when you keep pouring all you have into everyone else's cup? You can't. You have to quench your own thirst before you can

PLEASE

start helping all the other people who are begging you for a sip.

When you feel compelled to share, you share from your extra, from your overflow, and you only share what you can afford to give without depleting your own stores. This way, you aren't drained, and you give from a place of stability, abundance, and joy instead of giving from a place of lack. The more you fill yourself up, the more you have to give. Other people's "juiciness" is their responsibility, and you are not obligated to share yours with them.

We have to unlearn that our time, energy, attention, and resources are best spent when given to others, or that extending ourselves beyond our limit is some noble deed. The only reward for burnout and exhaustion is resentment.

You are not on Earth to be a mule or a martyr. Honor how much you can give before you are depleted and keep the rest for yourself. You have permission to pursue pleasure so you can fill yourself up before going to pour into everyone else that needs you.

Conquering the Fear of Emotion

There are some people who feel right at home diving deep into their feelings. There are many more who would much prefer not to deal with emotions at all. Which one of these people are you? Author and activist Toni Cade Bambara wrote, "…if your house ain't in order, you ain't in order. It is so much easier to be out there than in here." How are you avoiding the emotional work you need to

PLEASE

do to get your "house" in order? Why? Can you really be your best self if you are repressing and denying aspects of your experience, trying to pretend certain things don't exist? Feeling is part of the feminine aspect that every person has. It should be normal for people of all genders to express emotion without fear. However, to feel any emotion deeply other than hate, anger, insecurity, shame, and obligation is the complete opposite of what we've been socialized to believe.

Black people, specifically Black women, can sometimes have a tendency to describe the suppression of, or unconscious responses to, our pain and difficult emotions as "just the way we are," but this is another aspect of ourselves that radical self-care, through the centering of our pleasure, will help us unlearn. We are not born "hard" and unemotional. We are not naturally abrasive or dismissive or mean. We have been discouraged from expressing ourselves and our emotions every time we have been accused of having an attitude or being dramatic when we were simply sharing how we felt in the moment. We have experienced pain that caused us to move through the world unemotionally as a means of protection. We got so good at protecting ourselves this way that we began to take pride in it. That pain response made us feel strong and safe from the possibility of being hurt again. Pain has become a badge of honor for us, not because we healed and conquered it, but because our pain is proof that we have survived something that could have been the end of us. We want to remain

PLEASE

protected at all costs, so we cling to the part of us that makes us feel safe: the walls our ego put up to protect us. What happens when we are able to actually process and move through our pain? Who are we without it? The idea of letting go of something we have held on to for so long is terrifying. Who does it benefit for you to stay in your pain? Who is made better by you operating from a place of detachment and hardness, especially when there is so much beauty and strength to be had if you tapped into your pleasure?

It is not easy to sort through the darkest corners of ourselves, but it is necessary for understanding what we truly need in order to experience long-term satisfaction and joy. Doing this work may require you to remember how people, places, and things have caused you harm.

In the face of this discomfort, remind yourself that you will not drown in your emotions, no matter how deep they are. Be willing to get very intimate with your feelings, exploring them from all sides. Where did they come from? When did it start? How are they soothed? What do they need to be healed? Expressing your emotions ultimately allows you to get your needs met. Eventually, you wade through the depths and come out on the other side with new knowledge of how to prioritize and maintain your wellbeing.

PLEASE

Pleasure Principles

- You deserve a life that is satisfying, easy, peaceful, and full of joy.
- You cannot pour from an empty cup, but you are not required to pour from a full one, either. Share what you can spare and keep the rest for yourself.
- Self-soothing is a natural and necessary response, but it is not the same as true self-care.
- Release any guilt and shame you have about putting yourself and your wellbeing before anyone and anything else.
- Get comfortable with celebrating yourself and releasing stifling ideas of vanity and humility.
- Practice exploring your emotions so that you understand what you need in order to be satisfied and you can recognize joy when it comes.

The Power of Pleasure

CHAPTER THREE

PLEASE

III
The Power of Pleasure

How much better do your days seem to go when you feel good? How much easier and more often do you get what you need and manifest what you want when you are buzzing with joyful positivity? On the other hand, think about how much things just don't work and how much more frustrated you are when you're running yourself ragged and neglecting yourself. Society and its investment in work and productivity has trained us to require explanation or qualifiers for addressing basic human needs like rest, relationships, community, and fun. We are made to feel like we have to work until we have earned these things and even then, we have learned to convince ourselves that we don't need them because that time and energy could be spent being productive elsewhere.

The Pleasure Trinity

The Pleasure Trinity is my way of thinking about increasing and maintaining our wellbeing and creative energy through pleasure. Sexuality, spirituality, and self-care are what I consider to be the three

PLEASE

gateways or entry points to pleasure because they are the foundation of physical and emotional wellness and they often work together to create the satisfaction, joy, ease, and peace we seek. There's almost nothing that you can do for yourself that wouldn't fall into one of these three categories. When we get into a space of truly understanding and intentionally cultivating our sexuality, spirituality, and self-care, we develop our own personal power through pleasure. This power is what helps us to manifest, to get things done, and to release the stress and tension we walk around with on a daily basis.

    The topics and phrases underneath each gateway are things that you can practice on a regular basis to help you access your pleasure. Think about what personally brings you satisfaction and joy in the areas of sexuality, spirituality, and self-care. Across each of these points of pleasure, what are some things that you love, that make you feel good, that you can't wait to do every single day? Those things are going to improve your wellbeing and increase your power to manifest all that you desire and deserve.

PLEASE

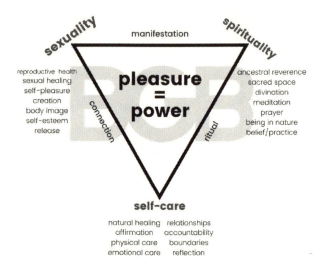

The Pleasure-Health Connection

Black women deal with the compounded stress of racism and sexism, and we are more likely than other women to experience major depression and general anxiety. We are subjected to stressful and upsetting topics and experiences in our everyday lives as well as in the media we consume — especially social media. Social media highlights other people mocking us, gaslighting us, displaying and finding entertainment in our trauma and abuse, praising of light and "exotic" women as the beauty ideal, and so much more. Our stress can also come from the way we are forced to be hyper-aware of how we are perceived, where we will be safe, and how people will treat us. Merely existing in the world is

PLEASE

stressful for Black women, and that stress has been linked to many life-threatening health conditions that make our bodies fight against itself and cause irreparable, sometimes fatal harm. Face masks and shopping sprees are not enough to help us withstand and combat this constant barrage of negativity that we are subjected to at every turn, at any given time.

Prioritizing pleasure means taking good care of yourself. It is a decision to live fully, and not just survive, but to thrive. It means doing what you need to feel as joyful and peaceful as you possibly can on all levels. It means doing for yourself what you would do for others. It means making sure that the proper boundaries and practices are in place so that you literally do not die. It means realizing that you deserve all the goodness that life has to offer, all the desires of your heart, and all the sweetness, softness, and deliciousness that you can stand.

Pleasure is an investment in your future self. What can you do right now that's going to bring you ease, comfort, and contentment and also allow you to ride that wave of good feeling in the coming hours, days, weeks, months, years? What can you do today that your future self will thank you for? What can you plan, imagine, or create that will shape a satisfying and joyful life for yourself and others? What steps can you take toward that future that feel good to you right now?

PLEASE

Relationships, Sex, and Pleasure

We most often associate pleasure with sex, likely because our sexuality is one of the few areas of our lives where centering ourselves and how we feel is acceptable. However, even in our sex lives, there are times where we do not prioritize our own satisfaction. Because we have not been taught to ask for what we want and expect to get it, we are often uncomfortable asking a partner to do something we like. During such a potentially enjoyable act, we still deny ourselves what we desire and deserve.

Our relationship to our sexual selves is a complicated one. It is often marred by the teachings from our youth about what "good girls" do or don't do, the internalized "dirtiness" of exploring ourselves sexually, unwanted and uncomfortable sexual experiences, and all the things we have to consider to ensure that we are engaging our sexuality in the healthiest and safest ways possible. Our beliefs and hesitations around sex and sexual pleasure tend to spread to our experience of nonsexual pleasure as well. We have inherited ideas that following our natural urges and doing things that feel good is wrong or even dangerous, and that we should do all we can to avoid that danger and do the "right" or "safe" thing.

Associating pleasure only with sex or romantic relationships can lead us to believe that we need another person for us to experience pleasure, which is untrue. We don't ever have to wait for someone else to give us pleasure. Pleasure is not contingent upon anything or anyone but

PLEASE

yourself. You make yourself feel good. You blow your own mind and make your own toes curl. To borrow a line from the esteemed songstress Jill Scott, you incite yourself to chorus. We can, however, engage in relationships that enhance our pleasure and wellbeing, romantic, platonic, and otherwise.

When we start to dream up our ideal partner or friend, we tend to imagine their personality traits, their interests, what they look like, maybe how much money they make and what they do for a living. We meet people who may check off a few of those boxes, but rarely do we meet anyone that checks off all of them. We may start to think that the person of our dreams doesn't exist so we settle for what we can get. This is because we are looking for what we desire in other people instead of looking for those things in ourselves and finding people who will help us improve and amplify our pleasure while we do the same for them. Challenge yourself to begin that dream of the perfect match with thinking about yourself and what you enjoy. Consider what you are looking for in a person that you can develop in yourself first. What would it look like for a partner or friend to simply support and assist you in all the ways that you pursue and experience peace, ease, and joy? What traits would that require?

Practicing Pleasure

Cultivating pleasure in your daily life is the ultimate form of consistent and effective self-care. Don't get caught up in the performance of pleasure. It doesn't

PLEASE

have to look a certain way. Do what works for you.

Before we get into specific ways to create and cultivate pleasure, we must practice and learn what pleasure feels like inside and outside of our bodies. The easiest way to begin this practice is to start with pleasure that you can perceive with your external senses. What can you see, smell, hear, taste, and touch that feels good? Run your fingers over your skin and note the sensation that arises. What scents do you love to linger in as long as possible? What food or drink instantly makes your mouth water and your body dance with delight? What makes you feel like humming or singing or shouting "YES!" at the top of your lungs? What makes you want to squeal and giggle? These are all experiences of pleasure, especially when they happen at the exact moment we are in need of rest, care, joy, or peace.

   Notice when and where you feel pleasure in your body. Your shoulders may drop and relax. Your heart may swell and feel full. Maybe you get goosebumps on your arms or the hair stands up on the back of your neck. Maybe you feel like you want to cry or laugh or scream some sound that only makes sense to you. You may even feel sexually aroused or other sensations in or around your vagina. These are indications of your body experiencing pleasure. When we know what pleasure feels like in our bodies, we can more easily determine the things that bring us more satisfaction and joy, and the things that do not.

PLEASE

Another way to practice getting in tune with your body, its needs, and its ways of communicating those needs is to practice different emotions so you know how they feel in your body. Try to make yourself happy or excited using a memory or a daydream that you conjure up. Try to conjure sadness, anger, even numbness or apathy. Note how these emotions feel in your body and where you feel them most. For example, your joy may make your head feel light and buzzy, and your sadness may make your chest or back feel squeezed or heavy. When you can acknowledge what you're feeling and where you are feeling it, you can better address your body's need for pleasure.

Pleasure requires that we frequently check in with ourselves and assess our wellbeing on every level — mind, body, and spirit. Ask yourself if you truly feel better and if your day-to-day experience of life is improving.

It is important to remember that while we are practicing radical self-care, pleasure may not always be the immediate sensation. When we need to have difficult conversations, break bad habits, disconnect from people, recognize and stop negative cycles, and other hard things so that we can feel better and be better, we may feel hurt, regret, shame, fear, and many other emotions before we get to pleasure. Radical self-care means acting in your best interest for your long-term wellbeing. In these moments, we must remember that we eventually will get through these emotions and find our way back to center while recreating the beliefs

PLEASE

we have about what we deserve and what we allow in our lives.

Pleasure Boosts

The next part of this chapter will outline a number of rituals that you can adopt to enhance your self-care practice, increase your pleasure, and as a result, increase your power. These practices are not in any particular order, and you can choose any combination of these that feel good to you. Remember: if it doesn't feel good, don't do it. You can use your comfort level with each exercise to measure how much you are progressing on your journey toward pleasure and self-care. But if something just doesn't do it for you, that's okay.

These are not one-and-done activities. They are not rigid in that they have to be followed exactly as written. You may personalize them and change them to suit your preferences and needs. By no means is this section exhaustive. You should create your own pleasure rituals that are meaningful to you. Consistency and intention are key!

There are additional resources and exercises in Part Two of this book.

Put Yourself First

Prioritizing yourself and your needs requires practice. When you are faced with a request on your time, energy, attention, or resources, practice pausing in the moment to ask yourself if this person,

PLEASE

place, or thing you're being asked to engage in makes you feel joyful. Does it excite you? Does it help you to grow and become a better person? Will it energize you, nourish you, or truly make you feel better? If the answer to most of these questions is "no," then you know this probably isn't something you should agree to. Sit with any feelings of guilt or anxiety you have about saying no to something. Where do these feelings come from? What are you afraid will happen if you say no?

On the other hand, we will all, at some point, find ourselves tasked with some necessary thing that we don't enjoy but must get done. In these moments, the best thing we can do for ourselves is to think about how to make the task as comfortable, easy, and joyful as possible. For example, maybe you are dreading doing your taxes. You could do them while sitting in your favorite place with a snack or drink you enjoy. If you are avoiding cleaning out your closet, turn on a playlist of your favorite music, a podcast you've wanted to listen to, or an audiobook you can get lost in as you work. Small additions of things that delight you can make a big difference.

If you are dealing with something that just cannot be made more fun (there are some tasks and obligations in life that are downright horrible), plan to treat yourself to something you enjoy directly after the task is complete. It is important to be able to restore your energy and return to your baseline of contentment, especially after doing something that is physically or emotionally draining.

PLEASE

What are you giving away that you need for yourself? What are you denying yourself that you need? Radical self-care is a lifelong practice of using your energy wisely and in ways that do not leave you depleted. Frequently check in and ask yourself what brings you joy and figure out how you can make that happen.

Building Boundaries

Boundaries are simply the way you choose to interact with the world and the ways that you will allow the world to interact with you. Boundaries help to keep out the things you know you don't enjoy so that you have room for all the things you want and need. Unfortunately, establishing and maintaining boundaries is one of the hardest parts of self-care because it requires us to stand firm in our desires, put ourselves first, and defend ourselves against those who try to cross the line, especially the people we love most.

You know your boundaries are weak or nonexistent when you feel the need to make other people feel good at the expense of your own happiness or comfort. The feeling of obligation to please others because you don't want them to be angry or disappointed with you takes away your right to ease and peace in your life. You do not have to allow people to treat you any old kind of way, regardless of their relationship to you. Your boundaries determine who and what gets to have access to you and the rules they must abide by to maintain access to you.

PLEASE

You cannot expect other people to know or enforce boundaries for you. No one is going to be checking on you to see if we have given too much. People will continue to ask of you and take from you as long as you continue to give. Very few people have the self-awareness to know when they have worn out their welcome with you. All the internal "Why don't they understand….?!" and "Why do they think….?!" and "Don't they know….?!" that you say to yourself when another person continues to cross your boundaries lets you know that they probably don't know where the line is with you, and you probably didn't establish it.

Establishing boundaries starts with figuring out what you have allowed from people, places, and things that has left you feeling exhausted, used, or hurt after the encounter. Be specific in naming how you felt — did you feel like you were taken advantage of? Did you feel unheard? Did you feel disrespected or embarrassed? What have you neglected or sacrificed in order to give of yourself to other people? While bringing up these emotions might be painful, you must name the feeling and identify the cause of that feeling in order to create the boundary that stops it from happening again.

Practice putting your boundaries into words so that you can let people know how to engage with you.

Boundaries sound like:

- "My work hours are 9:00am to 5:30pm. I will respond to your

PLEASE

email at my earliest convenience."
- "We can speak to each other respectfully or we won't speak at all."
- "I can help you find resources to assist you, but I cannot continue to lend you money."
- "The topic of (insert sensitive subject) is not up for discussion. Please do not bring it up again."
- "Please text me and ask if you can come over before showing up at my door."
- "I'm happy to hang out with you but I don't enjoy going to nightclubs. Let's do something we both enjoy to spend time together."
- "I don't want another; one drink is my limit."

- "Please check in with me to see how I'm doing before venting to me, as I may not be in a space to support you in the ways that you need."
- "I'd rather not hug, but we can shake hands."
- "I will only participate in this project if I am paid X amount for my time and skills."
- "I understand that you are upset, but you will not speak to me that way and maintain a relationship with me."
- "There are people attending the party that I'd rather not share space with, so I won't be going. Thank you for the invitation. Maybe we can grab coffee together soon."

PLEASE

- "I may not be working but that does not mean that I am available for anything I didn't plan for."
- "If my partner/children are not treated with respect, I will no longer attend family events."

Notice how these statements often start with or include "I" and "my." They also state a solution or alternative that you are willing to provide or participate in and an action that will be taken if your boundaries are not respected. Your boundaries are about what works for you and they do not have to accuse anyone of anything in order to explain how you will and won't engage with others. Develop healthy boundaries around every part of your life so that you and others know what your rules of engagement are. If it helps you to visually see where your boundaries are around different people, places, and things, create a "Want, Will, Don't, Won't" list to determine what you desire, what you are willing to accept, and your boundaries around what you dislike and will not accept. You do not owe anyone an explanation for the boundaries you put in place. Let your "no" stand on its own and if people are not open to accepting the alternative you offer, then you respond accordingly. Saying no to others is saying yes to yourself, and you deserve to do that without guilt or shame.

 It is important to consider whether the boundaries you establish are for your peace and wellbeing, or if they are a result of fear and pain that prevent you from growing. For example, if you are presented with a new opportunity and

PLEASE

your first thought is that you want to turn it down, think about if you want to turn it down because it doesn't align with what makes you feel good or if you want to turn it down because you're afraid you're not good enough and you might fail. Do you avoid certain conversation topics because they are mean-spirited and unproductive or because they bring up something you need to own and be accountable for? Understanding this distinction will let you know if you have set healthy boundaries that center your wellbeing.

    Maintaining boundaries requires bravery and commitment. If you don't take your boundaries seriously, no one else will. There are some wonderful people who will respect and abide by the boundaries you set because they care about your wellbeing, but there are many more who will still try to take advantage of you or believe that they should be an exception to your rules. These can be hard conversations to have, especially with people who believe that they should have unrestricted access to you because of their relationship to you. These are the people who may conveniently "forget" the boundaries you set or even be angry at you for daring to establish rules for your relationship. Their anger is not an indication that you have done anything wrong, but an indication of who does and does not have their own healthy boundaries or commitment to their own pleasure.

    When you start to put yourself first and live a joyful, peaceful, satisfying life, people will start to dislike you. They will

PLEASE

say you've changed, you're selfish, you're acting funny, and you're out of touch with reality. They will make up all kinds of things about you. They will accuse you of losing your mind or falling into the wrong crowd. They may say that you don't love or care about them because you won't do what they're asking you to do. When people say things like this, they are just lashing out because they are triggered. They are triggered because you are a shining reminder of their potential. They are uncomfortable because you are living in your truth and that is something that they have always wanted to do but instead they held on to personal pain and public perception. They are jealous, and that is none of your concern. Clear these people from your circle and keep on living. Pay attention to the people who support you in your efforts to maintain healthy boundaries, as these are the people who are meant to be in your life.

Practice sticking to your boundaries so that you maintain your comfort and peace without fearing backlash for standing up for yourself. You do not need to defend yourself or your rules of engagement. If you are struggling with feeling guilty for setting boundaries, remind yourself that you would rather be temporarily uncomfortable while respecting your own time and energy and protecting your peace than to sit in never-ending resentment and exhaustion. Your boundaries allow you to put more energy, more intention, and more power into the things that bring you joy.

PLEASE

Create Community

From the time we are born into this physical realm, we have found comfort in being seen, heard, and held by people who love us. That desire does not disappear once we grow up. Human beings are communal. We thrive when we are connected to others. Community care can be one of the most healing practices of self-care because it reminds us that we don't have to carry our burdens by ourselves; there is someone there to lean on until we can get back on our own two feet. Allowing others to love you and show that love through being by your side through life's ups and downs can provide joy, comfort, ease, and peace because we are reminded, through thoughts and actions, that we are not doing life alone.

Your community consists of the people you can rely on when you need a break from your kids, a night out on the town, a night inside on the couch, a pick-me-up after work, an extra hand to help around the house, or a hug and a shoulder to cry on. Your community can include family, friends, lovers, neighbors, and any other people that you can call on in times of celebration as well as times of need. Your community does not have to be large to be felt. If there are one or two people that can support and uplift you, then your community consists of one or two people. The size of your community is not necessarily equal to its strength.

Your community allows you to be exactly who you are. They should be a safe space for you to express what you need and allow people to rally around you to

PLEASE

make it happen, and you do the same thing for them. Within your community, you don't have to hear things like "you're so strong, you can handle it" or "you're always so confident, surely someone like you doesn't want/need (insert thing you desperately want and need here)." Your community, your people, allow you to be vulnerable and cared for while also affirming who you are and what you are capable of. They should be your biggest cheerleaders while taking care not to enable you in habits that do not serve your wellbeing. They should reflect all of your goodness back to you and help you elevate to your best, most radiant, and fulfilled self.

    Black women can often find it difficult to be in relationship with one another. Many of us have been socialized to believe that other women can't be trusted, but this can be unlearned. Audre Lorde said, "We have to consciously study how to be tender with each other until it becomes a habit because what was native to us has been stolen from us, the love of Black women for each other." Being in community with other people takes commitment and practice. If you are creating community from scratch, start by building relationships with people who you feel are trustworthy and compassionate. Be open to meeting like-minded people if you don't already have them around you. Seek to find common ground with new people you may be introduced to or had previously only been acquaintances with. An occasional text or phone call to keep in touch can get the momentum going. Take an active interest

PLEASE

in the people you'd like to be in community with and make sure that same affection and concern is reciprocated. Invite people you feel like you can trust to be a part of your life and pay attention to how they respond to your wants, needs, and boundaries. You'll know when you find someone who will be a long-standing member of your community. The vibes won't lie!

Keep in mind that in order to create and maintain community, the relationship must be balanced. No one wants to feel used. Everyone should have healthy boundaries in place to ensure they are giving to their community in ways that are meaningful and sustainable, while knowing that the community will show up for them when they need it.

Discover Your Self-Love Language

Most of us are familiar with our love language or the way we recognize and receive love. These languages include words of affirmation, acts of service, gifts, quality time, and physical touch. But if you were to apply the idea of love languages to your self-care practice, do you know what to do for yourself in order to feel loved and cared for?

Get familiar with how you show love to yourself in the ways that you can best receive it. It may not match the same ways that you prefer to receive love from a friend or romantic partner. For example, you may be delighted by acts of service when they come from a friend or partner but acts of service done by you and for you might sound like a terrible time.

PLEASE

Instead, you might feel loved when you have space to be alone or rest (quality time). You might feel loved best when you can treat yourself to something you've been wanting (gifts). Consider all the ways you can make these love languages meaningful in your own self-care practice and incorporate them into your regular routine.

Create Rituals

Rituals are simply routines that you establish that help you to restore your energy and bring you peace, comfort, and joy on the regular basis. From the time you wake up to the time you go to sleep, you are probably engaging in hygiene rituals, beauty rituals, food rituals, work rituals, and more. What if you could be more intentional in the way you move through the day, ensuring that you begin and end each part of your schedule with an activity that is pleasurable and restorative?

    Your rituals could look like writing your intentions for the day in your journal when you wake up and writing down five things you're grateful for in the evening right before bed. You could make a ritual of your body care, dressing yourself every morning and evening with lotions or perfumes that delight your senses. At work, you could make a ritual of spending the first twenty minutes of your day reading emails, listening to music, and drinking coffee or tea. Anything that feels grounding and positive to you, do that daily.

PLEASE

Go Play

Do you make time to just have fun? The need and desire for play doesn't end in childhood. Play not only increases our pleasure but it can create positive connections with ourselves, our loved ones, and our environments. Play also creates meaningful memories and could become a powerful ritual, especially when you are feeling like you are in need of rest or care. Laugh. Smile. Move. Have fun. Play is a reminder of our freedom to do with our bodies whatever we please.

What did you like to do when you were young? Don't be afraid to explore those childhood joys again. Find a swing set and go as high as you can. Play tag or hide and seek with your kids or your friends. Have a water gun fight or play the hand games you remember chanting on the playground in elementary school. Jump rope, swing from monkey bars, play a video game, or work on a puzzle. Be as silly as you want to be. Feelings of "I'm too old for this" will pass, especially once you really start having fun. No one is immune to the power of laughter and having a good time.

Treat Yourself

When we think about treating ourselves, we often think about something we don't often allow ourselves to have. We have a tendency to talk ourselves out of the things we desire most by thinking it's too expensive, it's a waste of time or money, you already have a functioning (insert

PLEASE

something old and falling apart here) so you don't need another one, if you take the time or spend the money something's going to come up and you're going to regret it, etc. What is really at play is the part of us that tells us that we are undeserving of what we want, and that we will be punished for getting or doing this thing for ourselves.

Define luxury for yourself. It doesn't have to include designer bags or five-star hotel stays. It doesn't even have to cost money. What can you do and have that makes you feel cared for, celebrated, beautiful, and satisfied? What can you treat yourself to that makes you feel like you are worthy of all of life's good things? Change your thinking around what it means to do and have nice things for yourself. Then, go do or get something nice for yourself.

Choose Your Feelings

You have the power to decide how you want to feel every day. Start by setting the intention for the feelings you want to experience that day. Do you want to feel beautiful? Abundant? Joyful? Healthy? Free? Energized? Cozy? Brave? Any feeling you want to feel is valid and available to you.

Once you decide how you want to feel, you can start to plan how you can attain this feeling throughout your day. Feeling exhausted and frazzled and want to feel cozy and comforted? You may decide to wear your softest sweater, spend a night cuddling a partner/friend/kid/pet on the

PLEASE

couch instead of going out, and turn your thermostat down so you can sleep with your warmest blanket. Not feeling well physically and want to feel healthy? You can make choices about what to eat, sign up for a dance class, call up friends to join you in a hike, or spend your evening playing outside instead of sitting on the couch. You could make yourself feel beautiful by dressing up and taking selfies or wearing your favorite lipstick for no particular reason other than because it looks amazing on you. These examples don't even begin to scratch the surface of the pleasure you can create around you. Great days don't have to be an exception or a surprise. You can intentionally plan them so they can be your new normal. All you have to do is make the decision and follow through.

Make Way for Rage

We live in a society that tells us that to feel or show anger is a bad thing. We are dismissed and not taken seriously when we are rightfully angry. We see people who don't show anger praised for being "mature," "intelligent," and "sophisticated." We're told that we will be listened to if we're calm, unaffected, and quiet. We are especially praised for "quiet strength" and seeming "unbothered." But we must make room for our rage.

Expressing our real emotions, no matter what they may be, is a step towards radical self-care for Black women. Science has proven that holding in anger can lead to heart disease and hypertension. To be able to be our truest selves, say what we need to say, do what we need to do, and move

PLEASE

through that energy so that we can get back to joy — this is an act of self-preservation. Do not allow yourself to be eaten up by all the things you didn't say, didn't do, and the guilt you have because we're taught that anger is a shortcoming of our character.

Anger is not poison; it is fuel. Use it. Honor your anger. Give it space. Let it breathe. You have the right to be angry until it runs out of steam. The balm of pleasure, the healing nature of satisfaction and joy will be that much sweeter on the other side of rage.

Practicing Forgiveness

Forgiveness in this context is about you, not about anyone else. If you want to be able to reap all the benefits of a life full of satisfaction and joy, you have to hold yourself accountable for the part you played in neglecting yourself and forgive yourself for the things you and your loved ones experienced as a result of you not being your best self, acting in your best interest, or prioritizing your wellbeing.

In my early twenties, I experienced a deep betrayal at the hands of a person I called my best friend. I didn't know what she had done until years after the actions had taken place, so by the time I found out and turned to other friends to vent, many people told me how they knew what was happening in the moment, and for whatever reason they had justified in their own minds, decided it wasn't their place to relay the information to me. I can admit now that I was stuck in victimhood for a few years after this. I was disappointed, I

PLEASE

was embarrassed, and I felt like I couldn't trust anyone, especially the people who knew I was being done wrong and didn't inform me.

I replayed various scenarios over and over in my mind, trying to figure out what I did to deserve everyone turning on me (in reality, no one "turned" on me, but this was the story I was telling myself). I was angered further when I would want to talk about the situation with people (for the millionth time) and they started to change the subject or avoid me altogether. Why didn't anyone care? Why didn't my other "friends" hate this person for hurting me like I would hate anyone who hurt them? Why didn't anyone stand up for me and defend my honor like I would have done for any of them? These are the questions that kept me up at night for longer than I'd like to admit.

All the symptoms of not being able to let go of this emotional pain surfaced in my body: anxiety attacks, insomnia, stomach issues, and more. The longer I sat with this hurt, the more I realized that the grudge I was holding was less about the person who wronged me and more about how I felt towards myself once I retraced all the connected events and saw how I missed (or ignored) the signs of what was going on. I chastised myself for not putting two and two together when it was right in front of my face. I regretted every time I saw something concerning but brushed it aside. At a certain point, I decided it was my own fault that my feelings were hurt. If I had just paid more attention and trusted my gut, maybe I

PLEASE

wouldn't have been caught off guard and maybe I would be in less pain. This made me feel even worse.

After a while, I got tired of feeling bad physically and emotionally and decided that if I felt like I was the one at fault for my hurt feelings, then I needed to forgive myself so that I could let this situation go and move on.

Here is a set of affirmations that I repeated nightly until my physical symptoms and emotional attachment to the situation disappeared:

I forgive myself for putting other people's wants and needs ahead of my own.

I forgive myself for expecting certain things from people that did not have it to give.

I forgive myself for punishing myself for things that were not my fault.

I forgive myself for what I overlooked.

I forgive myself for not trusting my intuition.

I forgive myself for not believing what I saw.

I forgive myself for what I didn't know.

I am proud of my resilience.

I am proud of my growth.

I am grateful and excited for new beginnings.

PLEASE

These affirmations did not immediately resonate or feel true to me, but I was consistent in repeating them. Whenever I started back down the path of victimhood or blaming myself, an affirmation would pop into my head and I would choose another thought that was more positive and based in reality. I believed that, eventually, I would subconsciously get through to myself and rewire my thinking about the situation and what was really hurting me. Once I was able to get past this hurt, I was able to use it as a lesson and detach from feeling like a victim. My return to pleasure required me to do the work of holding myself accountable for the things I could change, which was expressing forgiveness for the things that I could control but didn't. Whatever energetic returns befell the people who hurt me was none of my concern.

Nothing can change before forgiveness. Grudges and resentment, especially when held against yourself, keep your energy stagnant, which means you're not growing. What are you holding on to? Is the story you're telling yourself the true version of events? Are you blaming other people for decisions you made? What if you are not the victim? What are you not moving on from? Where do you need to be held accountable?

Rest

Do you feel guilty about taking a nap during the day? Do you believe you have wasted time if you have spent any extra time sleeping? Are you forcing yourself to stay awake because you have been taught that you only deserve rest when you work

PLEASE

hard? Let go of the idea that you have to earn rest. Rest is your restorative space, your time to bask in peace and ease as well as to dream and gain clarity, and you are allowed to engage in rest whenever you feel like it. Rest is one of the most deliberate forms of resistance and radical self-care in the face of a society that tells us we are only valuable when we are productive.

   Rest typically makes us think of sleeping, but it can also look like just closing your eyes for a few minutes, taking leisurely time with yourself and your daily rituals, or spending any amount of time not actively working or producing (or thinking about working and producing). Think about how you can rest on all levels of your being — physically, emotionally, mentally, spiritually, sensually, creatively, socially, etc.

Take afternoon naps. Spend the day in bed. Daydream at your desk. Allow yourself time for deep, uninterrupted nothingness. Enjoy a weekend with no work and no plans. All of your responsibilities and obligations will still be right there when you return from your rest. You do not have to wait until you are burnt out and exhausted to take a break. You deserve rest right now.

While you are crafting your pleasure practice, do not be alarmed if your needs change with life's circumstances. Some moments of your life may require more

PLEASE

rest and relaxation, while others will require movement and connection in order to get back to your natural state of ease, satisfaction, and joy. Along this journey, you may find that the things that used to satisfy you no longer do so. Don't be afraid to explore and add new practices to your pleasure toolbox.

    Beware of self-sabotage. We all have an ego that does the very important job of keeping us safe, letting us know what poses a threat to our wellbeing and what doesn't. Unfortunately, our ego can sometimes make us believe that something is unsafe just because it is new and uncomfortable. Ego tells us to go back to what we were doing before because it is familiar and it got us this far, so it must be safe. Safer, at least, than this scary new thing you're attempting.

Putting yourself first and following your bliss may take your ego into overdrive if it is something you've never done before. You will recognize your ego when you start to have thoughts about how you can't do it, you don't deserve it, you're going to fail, you're going to ruin your relationships, everyone is going to hate you and call you selfish, and on and on and on. You might begin to think that you can't care for yourself in this way because you don't have money or time or opportunity, but there is a free or low-cost way to access the tools and resources you need for whatever it is that you want to be, do, and have. Don't psyche yourself out. Along this journey, you must resist returning to old habits and ways of thinking because they feel more comfortable than the new things you are

PLEASE

embarking on. Do not allow your ego to make you fall back into neglecting yourself. Do not sabotage your pleasure. If you are truly having trouble fitting your pleasure in with the everyday tasks of your life, do not use this as a reason to quit. Look for ways to make your self-care practice work for you.

Author and coach Debrena Jackson Gandy said we must "refuse to be our own enemy." Be kind to yourself. Show yourself compassion as you navigate the journey toward radical self-care through pleasure. If it seems that your methods of self-care are not working and nothing is allowing you to experience joy or peace or comfort, deeper exploration of your needs may be warranted, perhaps with the help of a licensed mental health professional or advisor that you trust.

Now is a good time to reflect on the Pressure Points from Chapter One. How have your responses or beliefs changed so far?

_____

PLEASE

Pleasure Principles

- Spirituality, sexuality, and self-care work together to increase the peace, comfort, ease, and satisfaction in your life.
- Your relationship to pleasure has a direct connection to the state of your health and wellbeing.
- Know what the sensations of pleasure feel like in your body so that you know when you are experiencing it and when you are not.
- Do not let your sexuality be the only area of your life where you feel comfortable asking for what you want.
- Seeking professional help is encouraged for processing traumatic and painful events in your life.

Pleasure Activated

CHAPTER FOUR

PLEASE

IV
Pleasure Activated

Pleasure activates your power to create and manifest a life that you desire and deserve. When we pursue and prioritize our pleasure, we grow closer and closer to the highest visions of possibility for ourselves — the person we always knew was there but didn't know how to find. Secure in our pleasure practice, we can very easily achieve goals, have more clarity and creativity, and watch ourselves bring ideas to fruition almost effortlessly.

All of the most prolific and esteemed women have stories and quotes about unapologetically taking care of themselves. Consider the brilliance that our favorite writers, artists, and musicians create when they have taken time to rest, to play, and to engage in their own pleasure. You have the same ability to tap into your creative genius when you are well taken care of. We feel our best when we actively move towards those inner callings we have and start doing the things we always wanted to do. Women who have cultivated and prioritized their self-care through their pleasure practice can change the world.

Before Black Girl Bliss existed, before there was a mainstream self-care

PLEASE

movement, I had "follow your bliss" tattooed on my wrist, a couple of inches below my palm. I had typed it up in Microsoft Word in some italicized font that I thought was pretty, printed it out, and took it to the world's jankiest tattoo shop for it to be permanently written into my skin. I still am not sure what compelled me to get those three words, but they have served as a reminder throughout my life to always do the things that excited me and made me feel good. Prioritizing my joy and my peace has improved my health, my wellbeing, and my life in ways that I couldn't have possibly imagined. Let this book and its message be your reminder that the entire Universe shifts when you commit to your bliss.

Pleasure as Resistance

We cannot combat the systemic harm forged against us if we have not prioritized our personal needs. We cannot be of use to any movement if we are not well. Former First Lady of the United States Michelle Obama said that we have to plan our joy so that we know it is coming, especially in the midst of work, obstacles, and difficult days. Knowing how to bring ourselves joy is what will get us through the hard times and help us create the things we want to see in our lives and our communities. How will we witness the fruit of our labor if we are too tired, too sick, too anxious or depressed to experience it? We can use our power created through pleasure to create a world in which our wellbeing is prioritized,

PLEASE

where we are free to follow our bliss, and where we are not only encouraged but expected to pursue the things that bring us joy, living as our very best selves and helping others to do the same.

    Author and activist Angela Davis has remarked that few people in the Black Panther Party were taking time to care for themselves and that she wonders how different the movement could have been if leaders and members of the movement had prioritized self-care. She said, "Anyone who is interested in making change in the world, also has to learn how to take care of [themselves]." Imagine a world where our leaders and change-makers can bring their fullest and best selves to their lives and their work because they regularly practice radical self-care, setting that example for all who know them and all who come after them.

Pleasure as resistance and resilience practice looks like loving yourself and putting yourself first in the face of people, places, and things that don't love you. It looks like resisting the demands on your body, on your time, and on your mind. It denies the falsehoods perpetuated by puritanical patriarchy and capitalism. It reclaims agency and freedom over our lives when so many people and institutions try to tell us who we should be and what we should do to be considered respectable, worthy, valuable, or successful.

PLEASE

Destiny Fulfilled

Your work can bring you joy and satisfaction when you take the time to figure out your gifts, talents, and interests. What is your purpose in this life? What do you know you were put on Earth to do? Consider the ways you can provide meaningful contributions to the causes and communities you care most about through your passions. The idea of doing the work you were created to do, sustaining yourself and your desired lifestyle by doing something you enjoy, is radical in a society that denies Black women access, opportunity, and fair compensation. Imagine how drastically the world could shift if everyone operated in their zones of creative genius, doing work that brought them joy. Imagine how our concept of work and productivity could change. You can create that drastic shift in your own life by taking stock of the things you enjoy doing, the things you are good at, the communities you care most about, and how you can serve those communities with your skills. When you are doing *your* work — the things your mind, body, and spirit delight in — you realize that you no longer count the hours until the end of the day. You no longer live for the weekend or experience Sunday night anxiety. You might find that access, opportunity, and significant compensation seem to fall into your lap when you commit to walking in your destiny, the path that was created just for you to share your gifts with the world and be celebrated for them. Walking in your purpose and doing work that you love for

PLEASE

the people you care most about does not mean that you won't get tired. It does not mean that you won't need to engage in various methods of self-soothing and self-care on the regular basis. Your boundaries and pleasure practices still need to be prioritized so that you maintain the energy, clarity, and creativity you need to do what you love.

Revolution through Pleasure

Toni Cade Bambara said that it was the job of artists to make the revolution irresistible. As creators and designers of our lives and our immediate environments, how can we make necessary changes for ourselves, our loved ones, and our communities that feel good? How can we build relationships with each other and ways of being in our communities based on ease and joy? It is revolutionary to put yourself first, to take care of yourself first, and to refuse anything that does not bring you deep satisfaction, joy, and ease. Radical self-care goes directly against everything we have been taught about what it means to be a good person. How can you be revolutionary in the way that you create and live your life? What does it look like to raise children who are able to feel deeply, using their emotions to guide them to what feels good, safe, comfortable, and easy? What would it be like for children to have parents, aunts, cousins, teachers, and neighbors who model radical self-care? How incredible would it be to watch them come to understand their power, their boundaries, their desires, and their

PLEASE

pleasure, setting a healthy foundation for adulthood?

Once we allow ourselves to let go of societal expectations and violent internalized beliefs, we can see our truest selves come to light. We can begin to operate in new ways that allow us to laugh, rest, dance, and thrive in the ways that feel natural to us.

Pleasure Principles

- Pleasure gives us the energy to do all the things we've dreamed of doing, to act on the ideas that come to us, and pursue the goals and dreams we have for ourselves.
- We cannot combat the systemic harm against us if we have not prioritized our personal needs. We cannot be of use to any movement if we are not well.
- Operating in your pleasure and sharing your gifts helps to create endless possibilities for yourself and your community.
- Letting go of societal expectations on our time, energy, attention, and resources allows us to develop new ways of living and thriving in the world.

PLEASE

It is my prayer that you come away from this book understanding how pursuing and prioritizing pleasure is the key to caring for yourself in a way that truly empowers, strengthens, and restores you so that you have the energy you need to achieve every single dream you have for yourself and your life. I hope that this book sparks a movement of accountability and community for sisters and friends to ensure that everyone is cared for in all the ways they desire and deserve. Radical self-care — putting yourself and your needs first — is the complete opposite of everything that we have been socialized to believe makes us a "good" person. We must be patient with ourselves as we unlearn restriction, sacrifice, and neglect, and relearn how to communicate with our bodies, minds, and spirits to give ourselves what we need to be the sensual, radiant, creative, energetic beings we were created to be. Self-care takes practice so don't concern yourself with doing it perfectly. What you thought you knew about yourself will change. What worked before may not work the next time. Pay attention to what your triggers and mistakes have to teach you, and remember that all you can do is your best with the tools and understanding you have in the moment.

PLEASE

It is your divine responsibility to care for yourself, to honor your wellbeing, to step into your power, and to allow pleasure to fill every aspect of your life. When you have finished this book and taken from it all the knowledge and healing you need, pass this information down to your daughter, your sister, your niece, your cousin, or any other young people in your life as they journey to and through womanhood. Create a new story for the women of your lineage, one that speaks of joy and play and rest and ease. Pleasure gives us the energy to do all the things we've dreamed of doing, to act on the ideas that come to us, and pursue the goals and dreams we have for ourselves because we are no longer expending that energy on things that leave us exhausted and overwhelmed. We must continue to examine our beliefs that have led us to disconnect from who we are and what makes us feel good. We must remember that life doesn't have to be all struggle and strife; there is another way to live that we can actively move toward.

Trauma, anxiety, and ideas of scarcity have a profound effect on our physical and emotional wellbeing. We have the right to engage in whatever truly heals us, regardless of what anyone else might think about it. In the midst of all of life's twists, turns, obligations, inconveniences, frustrations, and tragedies, maintain pleasure as your priority, and watch everything else fall into place. The state and circumstance of your life will let you know how well you are engaging in practices that restore your energy or if you are engaging in things that deplete you.

PLEASE

If you have read this book, you have taken the first step. The ancestral mothers are smiling upon you and opening the way to more satisfaction and comfort than you could ever imagine. The next section of this book provides resources and activities to further guide you along your journey. As you continue to heal and grow, you will undoubtedly encounter new teachers and more advanced resources to take you to the next level.

Thank you for reading!

If you enjoyed this book, please share your thoughts in the form of a review on whatever platform you purchased this book from. Your reviews help other women make the decision to begin this journey to healing through pleasure. If you know someone who is struggling with self-care and needs more pleasure in their lives, please send them a copy of this book.

If you'd like to dive deeper into the ideas and activities outlined here, I invite you to explore the additional resources and services on the website. Visit **BlackGirlBliss.com** for more information.

May you always be satisfied.

PLEASE

PART TWO

please:

AFFIRMATIONS, MEDITATIONS, AND RITUALS

CHAPTER FIVE

PLEASE

V
Affirmations, Meditations, and Rituals

Here is a list of affirmations that you can use within a ritual or whenever you need to remember and affirm your right and responsibility to pursue and prioritize your pleasure and self-care. Feel free to modify them to fit your needs. Memorize them, repeat them daily, post them where you will see them often, or make a habit of writing them down in your journal nightly. Choose one or two phrases that really resonate with you to repeat to yourself throughout the day. Choose another one or two phrases that make you uncomfortable or bring up some unhealed feelings and sit with those thoughts so that you can process those emotions and begin making these phrases true for you.

- I am always worthy of pleasure.
- I deserve all that I desire.
- I am worthy of receiving all the good I give to others.
- It is okay for me to put myself first.
- It is okay for me to keep some of my energy for myself.
- I deserve my own time, effort, and attention.

PLEASE

- I can do, be, and have anything that I want.
- I am only engaging in what feels good.
- I will rest without guilt.
- When I take care of myself, everyone around me benefits.
- My body appreciates when I take the time to care for it.
- My mind appreciates when I take the time to listen to its needs.
- My spirit appreciates when I take the time to remember who I was created to be.
- The more I prioritize pleasure, the more joy, peace, and power I have.
- I am grateful for even the smallest pleasures every single day.
- Caring for myself is always a good use of my time.

- Self-care is productive. Pleasure is important.
- I welcome all the ways that life can surprise and delight me.
- My natural state of being is pleasure. I can always tap in when I need to.
- When it comes to my joy and satisfaction, mine is the only opinion that matters.
- My life feels good, and it is only getting better.
- Having fun is a necessity that I require every day.
- I am committed to my pleasure.
- I am learning to love myself better.
- No one has a right to say what brings me joy.

PLEASE

- I do not have to earn pleasure. It is my right and my responsibility.
- My pleasure is my priority.

Meditations

These prompts can be used to inspire your journaling sessions, or you can sit with these prompts in your mind and pay attention what comes up.

- What responsibilities and obligations are you using as excuses for why you don't or can't prioritize and pursue pleasure?
- What are you giving away that you need for yourself?
- Where in your life are you trying to fulfill your craving for pleasure through work, production, and achievement?
- How do you typically speak to yourself? What is the tone of voice and the language you use? Would

PLEASE

you speak to someone else this way? Why do you deserve to be spoken to in this manner?
- In what ways have you prioritized other people and their feelings over your own? Why do you believe you had to do that? What do you think would happen if you stopped doing that? Are these consequences real or imagined?
- How do you truly feel when you see other women prioritizing and celebrating themselves? Why do you think that is?
- When do you experience the most joy?
- What are you good at? What do you do that excites you? Where and when are you complimented for your abilities?

- How do ideas of vanity and humility show up for you? How do these ideas help or hinder your growth and your joy?
- Who in your life are you asking to see you, hear you, and care for you? Who in your life do you reciprocate this for?
- Who are the people in your life that you consider part of your community? Who are the people you thought were part of your community but have proven otherwise?
- When do you ask for what you want? Are you asking people who are willing and able to provide it for you?
- What does pleasure look like in each area of your life: family,

PLEASE

romance, home, work, friendships, finances, etc.
- Fill in the blank: When I feel (insert an emotion here), my body responds with _____. (Example: When I feel joy, my body responds with warmth in my cheeks and an urge to laugh.)
- Take note of the thoughts and sensations in your body when you imagine yourself:
   …being soft and vulnerable.
   …being visibly and audibly angry, especially in a public place like work or school.
   …not having it all together and not trying to create the illusion that you do.

...being kind to yourself, especially when you make a mistake.

...standing up for yourself, especially toward the people closest to you.

PLEASE

Your Pleasure Manifesto

Your life feels fun. You look forward to each and every day. You are energetic and have amazing clarity. You feel rested, present, centered, and joyful. Your day-to-day tasks are completed quickly and easily. You feel enthusiastic about the people you spend time with and pour your energy into. You engage in work and play that makes you feel good. Your loved ones get the best of you. You accept yourself as you are and thus accept others for who they are. You take nothing personally and extend grace and compassion to those who are disconnected from their bodies and their wellbeing. You protect your time, energy, attention, and resources by establishing strong boundaries, and you are unapologetic in enforcing them. You share your gifts with the world and are a shining example of joy, peace, and possibility for others. Your very being is revolutionary. You are a radical Black woman in pleasure.

PLEASE

Rituals

Here is a list of self-soothing and self-care activities to use when you're feeling some type of way.

- Spend at least three full minutes taking deep breaths in through your nose, filling your belly, pausing for a moment, and releasing the breath through your mouth.
- Drink plenty of water to stay hydrated.
- Be still and silent. Sit with yourself and daydream, listen to your own thoughts, and just be in your body.
- Curate your social media intake to only include things that bring you joy or take a social media break.

- Celibacy. Challenge yourself to find pleasure outside of sex.
- Solo sex. Challenge yourself to explore your sexual pleasure without a partner.
- Cook (or order) a meal for yourself that you really enjoy.
- Practice speaking your boundaries out loud.
- Move your body through dancing, stretching, hula hooping, or any other way that feels good.
- Write down your thoughts in a journal. If you don't know where to start, start by stating the obvious. Name the things you can see, smell, hear, taste, and touch. Where are you? How do you feel right now? Why do you feel that way?

PLEASE

- Clean your living space and do what you can to make it a space that you enjoy being in.
- Spend time with the people you love and who return that love back to you.
- Take yourself on a date as fancy or as casual as you would like.
- Create your Bliss List – a list of people, places, things, and activities that you know you enjoy so that you don't have to think too hard about what to do when you're in need of more joy or more peace.
- Put together a self-care plan with a consistent schedule of activities you want to make sure you do for yourself daily, weekly, monthly, etc.

- Adorn yourself with clothing, jewelry, makeup, body paint, or anything else that makes you feel beautiful.
- Practice receiving compliments and praise. Stand in the mirror, look yourself in the eye, and say something kind about yourself. Then only respond with "thank you" no matter what other chatter is happening in your brain. Do this until it no longer feels uncomfortable to hear and accept nice things about yourself.
- Find a cause you believe in and contribute your time or resources to it.
- Say "no." Cancel plans when you don't feel like going anymore. Don't be afraid of missing out.

PLEASE

- Find a way to make someone's day brighter just to see them smile.
- Spend time in nature or surround yourself with natural elements like fresh air and sunshine.
- Explore different methods of meditation that work for you.
- Develop a quick, meaningful mantra or affirmation to repeat to yourself throughout the day that makes you feel good.
- Daydream. Imagine your happiest self in your happiest place.
- Take a nap or go to sleep earlier than is socially considered "bedtime."
- Take a bath or shower. Stay in there as long as you possibly can.
- Create a playlist of music that makes you want to sing and dance.

- Reparent yourself. What did you need from the adults around you when you were little? How can you give that to yourself right now?
- Change your self-talk and speak to yourself the same way you would speak to someone you love dearly.
- Do something creative without worrying about being good at it.
- Do something that allows you to escape into someone else's world for a while. Read a novel or short story, watch a movie or TV show, or play a video game.
- Find ways to engage in the work that you enjoy most. It may not be your day job, but if it fills you up and brings you joy, find time for it on a regular basis.

PLEASE

- Change your surroundings, even if it's just for a little while. Go somewhere you don't usually go where you can experience something that brings you pleasure.
- Treat yourself to something you consider luxurious.
- Create a Greatest Hits list by writing down all your accomplishments and things you are proud to have created or completed from as far back as you can remember. Update this list regularly!

Resources

CHAPTER SIX

PLEASE

VI
Resources

Book Club Guide

Starting a book club with your sister circle or any other supportive and like-minded group of women can help you to work through the concepts outlined throughout this book. These discussions should be safe spaces where participants know that what they share in the space will be held in confidence. In this section, you will find discussion points, activities for each chapter, and suggested reading for further study. You can choose to read through the chapter together or to come to the book club session having already read. The ideas outlined here are just a starting point. Feel free to create your own discussions and activities around the concepts of the book.

PLEASE

Session One: History and Context

Reading: Chapter 1 — "Start Here"

Opening: Have each person share what they hope to understand or solve by reading this book. Set the intention for the collective to receive all that they need and be led to their highest good through the collective study of this book.

Discussion Questions:
- Who was the first person to model self-care for you?
- Why do you participate in things that do not bring you joy?
- Before reading this chapter, did you only associate the idea of pleasure with sex? Why or why not?

Final Reflections: Where in your life do you recognize the denial of pleasure? What ideas of self-care did you have before and after reading this chapter?

Homework: Write down your responses to the questions from the very first paragraph of the book ("See yourself in your mind's eye…"). Create a visual representation of that version of you — a collage, drawing, painting, etc.

PLEASE

Session Two: Acknowledgement

Reading: Chapter 2 — "Permission Granted"

Opening: What have the Pressure Points brought up for you so far? Share with the group if you are comfortable doing so.

Discussion Questions:
- How have ideas around respectability and what is socially acceptable influenced your connection to your body and both your sexual and non-sexual pleasure?
- What have you been told you have to do, be, or have in order to be worthy of good things?
- Where in your life have you

realized that you distrust or avoid your own emotions? Why? How does that affect your relationship to yourself?

Final Reflections: Your joy and peace are valuable. What are you willing to do to make sure that you always have them?

Homework: Journal what you currently believe about self-care and pleasure. Reflect on what comes up that surprises you.

PLEASE

Session Three: Power and Praxis

Reading: Chapter 3 — "The Power of Pleasure"

Opening: Did you practice feeling pleasure as well as various other emotions in your body? Did anything about this exercise surprise you? Did any sensation feel foreign? What sensations felt familiar?

Discussion Questions:
- Which of the pleasure boosts seems like it would be easiest for you? Which of them seem most difficult? Why?
- How can you realistically and consistently create space for pleasure in your life?
- Where do you recognize that you

are sabotaging your wellbeing?
Why do you think that is?

Final Reflections: What does it look like for you when your pleasure (and subsequently, your power) is increased?

Homework: Create your Bliss List — a list of places, things, and activities that you can tap into when you are in need of comfort, joy, and peace.

PLEASE

Session Four: Activation

Reading: Chapter 4 — "Pleasure Activated"

Opening: What are some of the ways that you can use your increased personal power to have a positive influence in the world?

Discussion Questions:
- Are you fulfilling your destiny? How do you know? Why or why not?
- How do you plan to share the power of pleasure with the next generation?
- What would you love to see change about your community or society as a whole because of

more people engaging in radical self-care through pleasure?

Final Reflections: How have your responses to the Pressure Points changed since starting the book? What do you realize now that you didn't realize before?

Homework: Find a Pleasure Partner — someone who understands that you are trying to enhance your wellbeing and personal power through increasing and maintaining your satisfaction, joy, ease, comfort, and peace. Allow them to hold you accountable for caring for yourself in all the ways that you deserve.

PLEASE

Sources, Inspiration, and Suggested Reading

- **Got2BOshun** (Got2BOshun.org) by Iyalosa Osunyemi Akalatunde

- **Your Next Level Life** by Karen Arrington

- **Pleasure Activism** by adrienne maree brown

PLEASE

- F*ck That Cape: The Grown Woman's Unapologetic Guide to Putting Herself First
  by Jennifer Arnise

- This is Woman's Work: Calling Forth Your Inner Council of Wise, Brave, Crazy, Rebellious, Loving, Luminous Selves
  by Dominique Christina

- Women Who Run with the Wolves: Myths and Stories of the Wild Woman Archetype
  by Clarissa Pinkola Estés, Ph.D.

- All the Joy You Can Stand: 101 Sacred Power Principles for Making Joy Real in Your Life
  by Debrena Jackson Gandy

- Sacred Pampering Principles: An African-American Woman's

Guide to Self-Care and Inner Renewal by Debrena Jackson Gandy

- **The Nap Ministry: Rest as Resistance** by Tricia Hersey

- **Sisters of the Yam: Black Women and Self-Recovery** by bell hooks

- **A Return to Pleasure** by Rashida KhanBey Miller

- **The Desire Map: A Guide to Creating Goals with Soul** by Danielle LaPorte

- **Sister Outsider** by Audre Lorde

- **Shaping the Shift Podcast** by Thea Monyeé

PLEASE

- **The Body is Not an Apology: The Power of Radical Self-Love** by Sonya Renee Taylor

- **Own Your Glow: A Soulful Guide to Luminous Living and Crowning the Queen Within** by Latham Thomas

- **The Happy Black Woman Podcast** by Rosetta Thurman

- **Blessing Manifesting** (blessingmanifesting.com) by Dominee Wyrick

PLEASE

BLACK GIRL BLISS
is an educational platform dedicated to cultivating the spiritual, sexual, and self-care practices of Black women and femmes.

Learn more at **BlackGirlBliss.com**

Made in the USA
Middletown, DE
26 October 2022